first book of
cats

Isabel Thomas

D1355365

A & C BLACK
AN IMPRINT OF BLOOMSBURY
LONDON NEW DELHI NEW YORK SYDNEY

Published 2014 by
A&C Black
An imprint of Bloomsbury Publishing Plc
50 Bedford Square, London, WC1B 3DP

www.bloomsbury.com

ISBN 978-1-4729-0398-3

Printed in China by Leo Paper Products, Heshan, Guangdong

10 9 8 7 6 5 4 3 2 1

Contents

Cats

Cats are amazing animals. Look out for pet cats climbing and jumping as they explore outdoors. Watch them grooming their fur. Listen out for their purrs and miaows.

You can spot cats in towns and cities, in the countryside, and at cat shows. This book will help you to name the different breeds you see. It shows you some special features to look out for.

At the back of this book is a Spotter's Guide to help you remember the cats you spot. Tick the breeds off as you see them. You can also find more about different colours and patterns.

Turn the page to find out all about cats!

Abyssinian

Abyssinians look like the famous cats in Ancient Egyptian paintings. Look out for their special 'ticked' coats. This means every hair has two or three different colours.

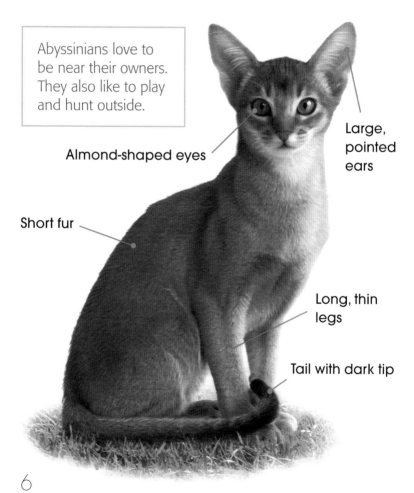

Abyssinians love to be near their owners. They also like to play and hunt outside.

Almond-shaped eyes

Large, pointed ears

Short fur

Long, thin legs

Tail with dark tip

American Curl

These cats are famous for their curled-back ears. They are very popular in the USA, but harder to spot in the UK.

Look out for Scottish Folds too. These cats have ears that curl forwards.

Ears curled back

American Curls can have kittens with curled or normal ears.

Short, thick legs

American Shorthair

American Shorthairs have larger bodies and longer legs than other shorthaired cats.

Ears with round tips

This cat has a tortoiseshell coat. Tortoiseshell cats are nearly always female.

Large, wide eyes

Powerful body

American Wirehair

These cats have coiled, springy fur. Stroking an American Wirehair feels a bit like stroking a lamb.

Like most cats, an American Wirehair's coat has three types of hairs. They are called guard hairs, awn hairs, and down hairs.

Wavy whiskers

Frizzy fur

Purrs all the time

Asian Bombay

Bombay cats are famous for their gleaming golden eyes and jet-black coats. Even their nose and paw pads are black. Bombay cats purr very loudly when they are happy.

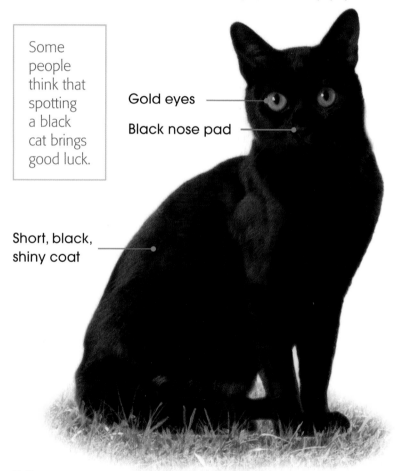

Some people think that spotting a black cat brings good luck.

Gold eyes

Black nose pad

Short, black, shiny coat

Asian Burmilla

These cats have the body of a Burmese with the coat of a Chinchilla. They are gentle and friendly cats that love to play with everyone they meet.

Female Burmillas are much smaller than males.

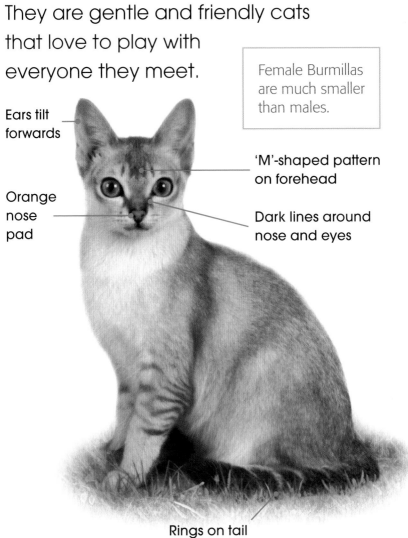

Ears tilt forwards

Orange nose pad

'M'-shaped pattern on forehead

Dark lines around nose and eyes

Rings on tail

Australian Mist

These friendly cats love to be stroked and cuddled. They even get on well with dogs. Australian Mist cats originally came from Australia. Today they are popular pets around the world.

Large, green eyes

Cream coat with spotted or marbled patterns

Plump, furry tail

Bengal

Bengals are pet cats that look like wild Asian Leopard Cats. They like having adventures and are frightened of nothing. Bengals even like playing with water.

Round eyes

Dark spots on a light coat

Front legs longer than back legs

Large paws

Birman

Birmans look like longhaired Siamese cats. Spot one by looking for the white 'gloves' on each paw.

Birmans have pale coats with darker fur on their ears, face, legs, and tail.

Dark points

Very bushy tail

Sapphire-blue eyes

Paws with white gloves

British Shorthair

These clever cats love
to roam around outdoors.
They are popular pets.
British Shorthairs can be
almost any colour and pattern.

Most British
Shorthairs have
copper, orange,
or gold eyes.

Big, round eyes

Large head

Small ears

Round cheeks

Short nose

Short fur

Short, strong legs

Large, rounded paws

Burmese

Burmese cats are clever, friendly, and love to have fun. They like to explore new objects by licking and chewing them.

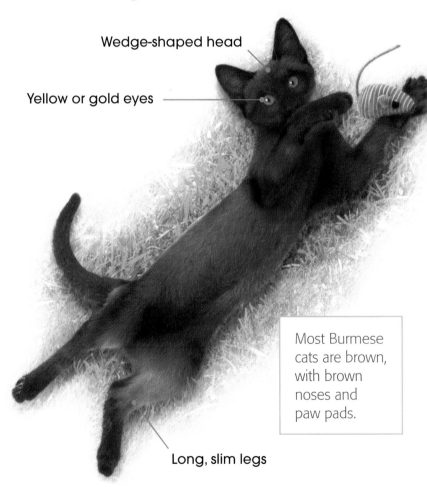

Wedge-shaped head

Yellow or gold eyes

Most Burmese cats are brown, with brown noses and paw pads.

Long, slim legs

Chartreux

Blue cats have been bred in France for hundreds of years. The first Chartreux cats were kept by monks in the Middle Ages.

Many Chartreux cats can purr, but can't miaow.

Gold, copper, or orange eyes

Round, wide head

Grey-blue coat

Chartreux cats look very similar to blue British Shorthairs.

Short, thick tail

Cornish Rex

Rex cats are famous for their wavy coats. Cornish Rexes are cheeky and love to explore. When they get tired, they find the warmest place in the house to curl up.

Rex cats are named after a type of rabbit with curly fur.

Small body

Large ears

Short, wavy fur

Short whiskers

Devon Rex

Devon Rexes have wide cheeks and enormous ears. Some people think they look like pixies or aliens! They are nicknamed 'poodle cats'.

Wide cheeks

Very large ears

Short whiskers

Short, wavy fur

Thin tail

Most cats wag their tails to show they are upset. Only Devon Rexes wag their tails when they are happy.

Domestic Longhair

Domestic Longhair cats are moggies with long fur. A 'moggie' is a cat whose family tree hasn't been recorded. They are also known as 'non-pedigree' cats.

Soft, thick coat

A moggie may have features from several different breeds.

Domestic Shorthair

These moggies look like British or American shorthairs. Their short coats often have a tabby pattern.

The markings on a tabby cat's forehead look like the letter 'M'.

Green or yellow eyes

Tabby cats have patterned coats like wild cats. Patterns help wild cats to stay hidden when they hunt.

Tabby coat

Egyptian Mau

Cats that looked like the Egyptian Mau were worshipped in Ancient Egypt. They were so important they were turned into mummies when they died.

Egyptian Maus can run faster than any other pet cat.

Light-green eyes

'M'-shaped marks on forehead

Brown or black spots

European Shorthair

European Shorthairs have thinner, less rounded bodies than British Shorthairs. They are related to the cats Roman soldiers kept to catch rats.

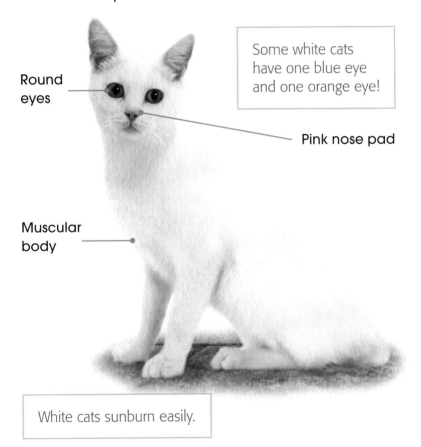

Round eyes

Some white cats have one blue eye and one orange eye!

Pink nose pad

Muscular body

White cats sunburn easily.

Exotic Shorthair

These cats look like Persian cats
with short coats. They are as gentle
as longhaired cats, but need less
brushing and combing.

Exotic shorthairs
have a quiet,
squeaky miaow
like Persian cats.

Large, round head

Small ears

Short nose

Short neck

Medium or
large body

Soft coat

Japanese Bobtail

Have you ever seen a cat waving hello? Japanese Bobtails are famous for sitting and raising one paw. They are known as 'beckoning cats'.

Japanese Bobtails have a short, curled tail that looks like a rabbit's puff.

Large, oval eyes

Short, curled tail

Korat

You might spot Korat cats in hot countries. In Thailand they are known as 'good luck cats'. Owning a Korat is thought to make you rich, happy, and healthy.

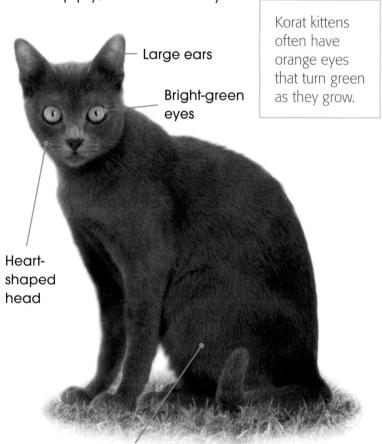

Large ears

Bright-green eyes

Korat kittens often have orange eyes that turn green as they grow.

Heart-shaped head

Grey-blue coat that shimmers

Maine Coon

These huge, friendly cats have long fluffy tails like raccoons. A Maine Coon's coat gets thicker in winter, to keep it warm. The longest hairs moult (fall out) in the spring.

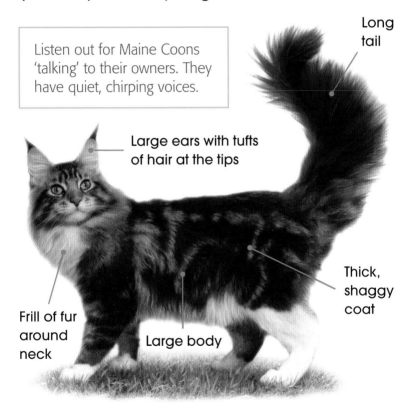

Listen out for Maine Coons 'talking' to their owners. They have quiet, chirping voices.

Long tail

Large ears with tufts of hair at the tips

Thick, shaggy coat

Frill of fur around neck

Large body

Many Maine Coon cats have a tabby coat.

Manx

Many Manx cats are born without a tail. They are also famous for acting like dogs. Manx cats love to chase balls and fetch toys. They can even learn tricks.

The first Manx cats came from the Isle of Man, an island in the UK.

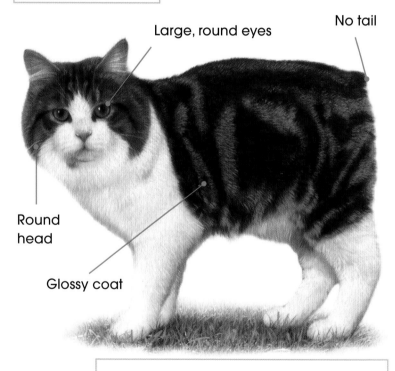

No tail

Large, round eyes

Round head

Glossy coat

Manx cats make chirping sounds as they brush their bodies against people they like.

Norwegian Forest Cat

The first Norwegian Forest Cats worked on farms in Scandinavia. They are very good at catching mice and rats. Their thick fur keeps them warm in cold winters.

These cats may be the 'troll cats' or 'fairy cats' from old Viking stories.

Thick coat

Ruff

Norwegian Forest Cats love fishing in shallow water.

Strong legs

29

 # Ocicat

Have you ever seen a spotty cat? Ocicats were named after a spotted wild cat called an ocelot. Their spots get darker as they grow older.

The first Ocicat was bred by accident.

Large pointed ears

'M'-shaped mark on forehead

Dark spots

The backs of a cat's eyes work like mirrors. This is why their eyes seem to shine in the dark.

Oriental Shorthair

Oriental Shorthairs have faces and bodies like Siamese cats. The difference is that their colour or pattern covers their whole coat.

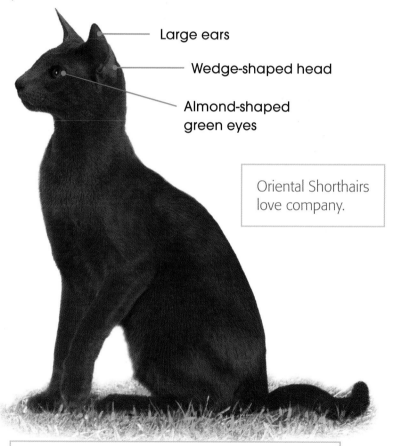

Large ears

Wedge-shaped head

Almond-shaped green eyes

Oriental Shorthairs love company.

This type of Oriental Shorthair is called a Havana.

Persian

Longhair cats are also called Persians. Their fluffy fur can grow as long as your hand. Persians are hard to spot. These gentle cats like to stay inside.

Persian cats come in more than 60 different colours and patterns.

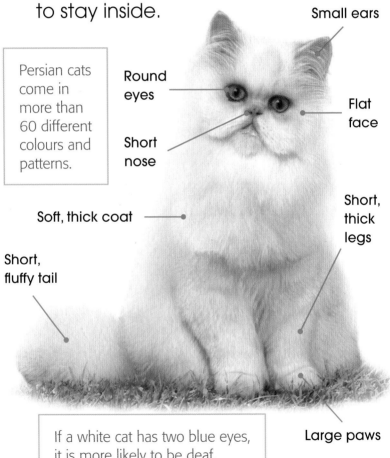

Small ears

Round eyes

Flat face

Short nose

Soft, thick coat

Short, thick legs

Short, fluffy tail

Large paws

If a white cat has two blue eyes, it is more likely to be deaf.

Ragdoll

These large cats do something strange when you pick them up. Their bodies go floppy like a ragdoll! Nobody knows why.

This is a bicolour Ragdoll. Bicolour cats have white fur on their tummies and legs.

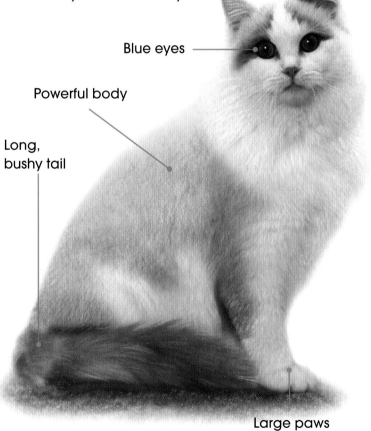

Blue eyes

Powerful body

Long, bushy tail

Large paws

Russian Blue

These cats have blue-grey coats that shimmer like silver. Their soft fur is so thick that stroking it leaves handprints.

If you spot a Russian Blue, listen carefully for its very quiet miaow.

Bright-green eyes

Long body

Long tail

Long legs

Siamese

Siamese cats have pale coats, with darker fur on their face, ears, legs, and tail. These cats like lots of attention. Jealous Siamese cats make a loud noise that sounds like a baby crying!

The first Siamese cats came from South East Asia. They are known as 'moon diamond' cats.

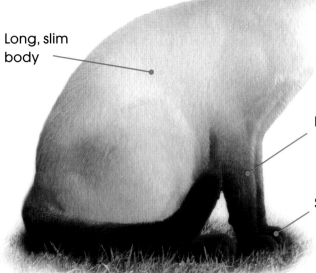

Large ears

Bright-blue eyes

Long, slim body

Long legs

Small feet

Somali

Somalis are nicknamed 'Fox Cats'. They have shaggy coats and bushy tails. Like foxes, they are clever and love to explore outdoors.

Tufts of hair on ears

Somali cats often look like they are smiling.

Ticked fur

Long, bushy tail

Sphynx

Sphynx cats are hard to spot. They have to live indoors. They have no furry coat to keep them warm, or protect them from the sun.

Stroking a Sphynx feels like stroking the skin of a peach.

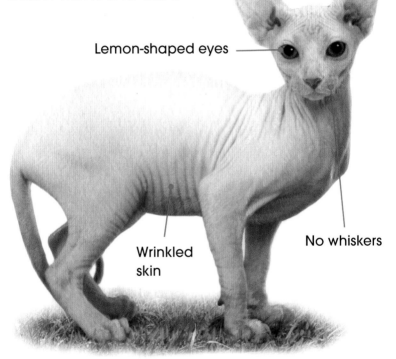

Large ears

Lemon-shaped eyes

Wrinkled skin

No whiskers

A Sphynx needs a bath every week to keep its skin clean.

Tonkinese

The first Tonkinese cats were the kittens of Siamese and Burmese parents. Can you spot features from each breed?

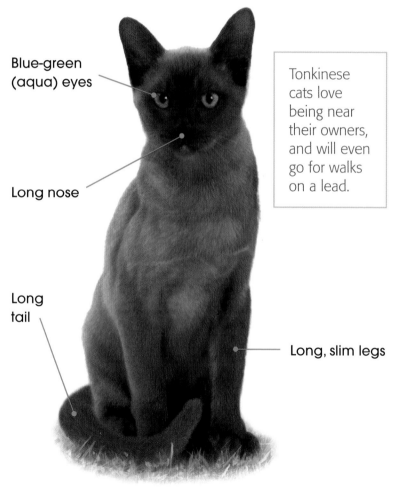

Blue-green (aqua) eyes

Long nose

Tonkinese cats love being near their owners, and will even go for walks on a lead.

Long tail

Long, slim legs

Toyger

Imagine seeing this animal strolling down your street. Don't worry – it's just a toyger! These pet cats are bred to look like tiny tigers.

Real tigers are fifty times bigger than a Toyger.

Long tail

Dark stripes

Orange coat

White chest and belly fur

Turkish Van

These cats love going for a swim. If there are no streams or ponds nearby, Turkish Vans will jump into baths or even toilets!

White blaze on forehead

Turkish Vans are named after Lake Van in Turkey.

Coloured fur on head, ears, and tail

White coat

Long, bushy tail

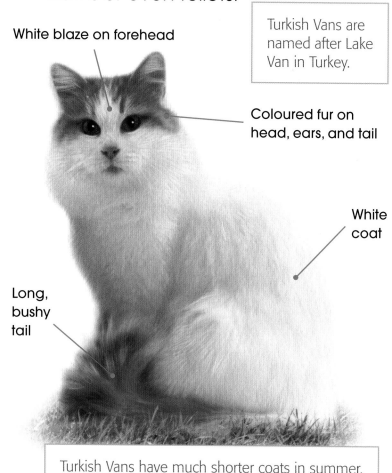

Turkish Vans have much shorter coats in summer.

Colours and patterns

 Self or solid cats have hair of just one colour all over their bodies.

 Bicolour cats have a white belly and legs, with patches of coloured fur on their head and back.

 Harlequin cats are black and white bicolour cats.

 Tortoiseshell cats have patches of red and black fur.

 Tortie-and-white cats have tortoiseshell coats with patches of white fur.

 Tabby cats have a coat pattern like wild cats. Some have stripes and some have blotches or spots.

 Colourpointed cats have a light coat, with darker fur on their face, ears, paws, and tail.

 Van pattern cats have white fur with patches of red or cream fur on their heads and tails.

Spotter's guide

How many of these cats have
you seen? Tick them when you
spot them.

☐ Abyssinian
page 6

☐ American
Curl
page 7

☐ American
Shorthair
page 8

☐ American
Wirehair
page 9

☐ Asian
Bombay
page 10

☐ Asian
Burmilla
page 11

☐ **Australian Mist**
page 12

☐ **Bengal**
page 13

☐ **Birman**
page 14

☐ **British Shorthair**
page 15

☐ **Burmese**
page 16

☐ **Chartreux**
page 17

☐ **Cornish Rex**
page 18

☐ **Devon Rex**
page 19

Domestic Longhair
page 20

Domestic Shorthair
page 21

Egyptian Mau
page 22

European Shorthair
page 23

Exotic Shorthair
page 24

Japanese Bobtail
page 25

Korat
page 26

Maine Coon
page 27

Manx
page 28

Norwegian
Forest Cat
page 29

Ocicat
page 30

Oriental Shorthair
page 31

Persian
page 32

Ragdoll
page 33

Russian Blue
page 34

Siamese
page 35

Somali

Sphynx

Tonkinese

Toyger

Turkish Van

Useful words

Chinchilla a silver-coloured Persian cat

kitten a baby cat

longhair a cat with long, fluffy fur

moggie another name for a non-pedigree cat

moult when hairs fall out, and a cat's coat gets thinner

non-pedigree a cat that is not pure bred, whose family tree has not been recorded

nose pad the small patch of skin on a cat's nose

pedigree a cat that is pure bred, whose family tree has been recorded

shorthair a cat with short, thick fur

ticked a coat where every hair has bands of two or three different colours

Find out more

If you would like to find out more about cats, start with these websites. You will discover where to visit a cat show, and how to care for pet cats.

The Governing Council of the Cat Fancy
www.gccfcats.org

The International Cat Association
www.tica.org/

Cats Protection: Cats for Kids
www.cats.org.uk/cats-for-kids

RSPCA Pet Care Guides
www.rspca.org.uk/allaboutanimals/
pets/cats